is for
Vulnerable

is for

Vulnerable

LIFE OUTSIDE THE COMFORT ZONE

Seth Godin

Illustrated by HUGH MACLEOD

PORTFOLIO / PENGUIN

PORTFOLIO / PENGUIN

Published by the Penguin Group

Penguin Group (USA) Inc., 375 Hudson Street, New York, New York 10014, U.S.A. • Penguin Group (Canada), 90 Eglinton Avenue East, Suite 700, Toronto, Ontario, Canada M4P 2Y3 (a division of Pearson Penguin Canada Inc.) • Penguin Books Ltd, 80 Strand, London WC2R 0RL, England • Penguin Ireland, 25 St. Stephen's Green, Dublin 2, Ireland (a division of Penguin Books Ltd) • Penguin Group (Australia), 707 Collins Street, Melbourne, Victoria 3008 Australia (a division of Pearson Australia Group Pty Ltd) • Penguin Books India Pvt Ltd, 11 Community Centre, Panchsheel Park, New Delhi – 110 017, India • Penguin Group (NZ), 67 Apollo Drive, Rosedale, Auckland 0632, New Zealand (a division of Pearson New Zealand Ltd) • Penguin Books, Rosebank Office Park, 181 Jan Smuts Avenue, Parktown North 2193, South Africa • Penguin China, B7 Jaiming Center, 27 East Third Ring Road North, Chaoyang District, Beijing 100020, China

Penguin Books Ltd, Registered Offices:
80 Strand, London WC2R 0RL, England

First published in 2012 by Portfolio / Penguin,
a member of Penguin Group (USA) Inc.

10   9   8   7   6   5   4   3   2   1

Copyright © Do You Zoom, Inc., 2012
Illustrations copyright © Gapingvoid Ltd., 2012
All rights reserved
Library of Congress Cataloging-in-Publication Data

Godin, Seth.
V is for vulnerable : life outside the comfort zone / Seth Godin ; illustrated by Hugh MacLeod.
p.   cm.
ISBN 978-1-59184-610-9
1. Success in business—Miscellanea. 2. Creative thinking—Miscellanea.
3. Alphabet books. I. MacLeod, Hugh, 1965– II. Title.
HF5386.G556 2012
650.1—dc23   2012037953

Printed in the United States of America
Set in Walbaum
Designed by Daniel Lagin

In memory of my mom, in honor of my dad, and for my kids

Seth Godin

These drawings are dedicated to my nephews and nieces, all five of them. May these words resonate with you one day, and God forbid that they never do. Lots of Love from Uncle Hugh :)

Hugh MacLeod

SEE THE WORLD THE WAY AN ARTIST DOES.

The Lorax makes me cry. Every time.

Dr. Seuss made me giggle when I was three. He taught me how to read when I was five. Today, he reminds me of how important our future is, whether or not we have kids.

Every one of his books is incredibly simple, some with just three hundred words inside. But the ideas stick with us, and even more powerfully, push us to take action, to embrace opportunity, not to merely watch and wait.

I'm hoping that this book I created with Hugh MacLeod will help you choose to see the world differently. Radically differently. I'm hoping that instead of asking, "How can this book help me do a better job to keep the world as it is?" perhaps you can momentarily choose to see the world as a different place altogether.

I'm trying to get under your skin. I'm trying to get you to stop being a spectator and a pawn in the industrial system that raised us, and maybe, just maybe, to stand up and do something that scares you. I want you to do what you're meant to do, what we're all meant to do, which is the hard work of creating art.

The artist wonders, "How can I break this?" and "Is it interesting?"

Go break something.

—Seth Godin

P.S. Read this book out loud to someone you care about.

ANXIETY is experiencing failure in advance. Tell yourself enough vivid stories about the worst possible outcome of your work and you'll soon come to believe them. Worry is not preparation, and anxiety doesn't make you better.

BIRL that log. Find your balance by losing it, and commit to feet in motion until you're birling and the log is spinning. The log isn't going to spin itself, you know. A spinning log is stable for a while, but not forever. That's why birling is worth watching.

COMMITMENT is the only thing that gets you through the chasm. Commitment takes you from "that's a fine idea" to "it's done." Commitment is risky, because if you fail, it's on you. On the other hand, without commitment, you will fail, because art unshipped isn't art.

DANCE with fear. Dance with done. Dance with the resistance. Dance with each other. Dance with art.

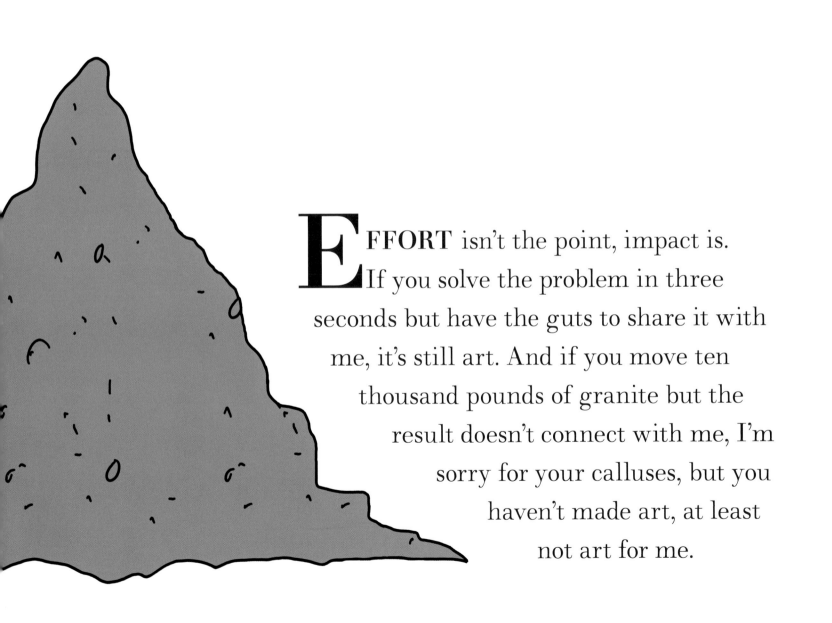

EFFORT isn't the point, impact is. If you solve the problem in three seconds but have the guts to share it with me, it's still art. And if you move ten thousand pounds of granite but the result doesn't connect with me, I'm sorry for your calluses, but you haven't made art, at least not art for me.

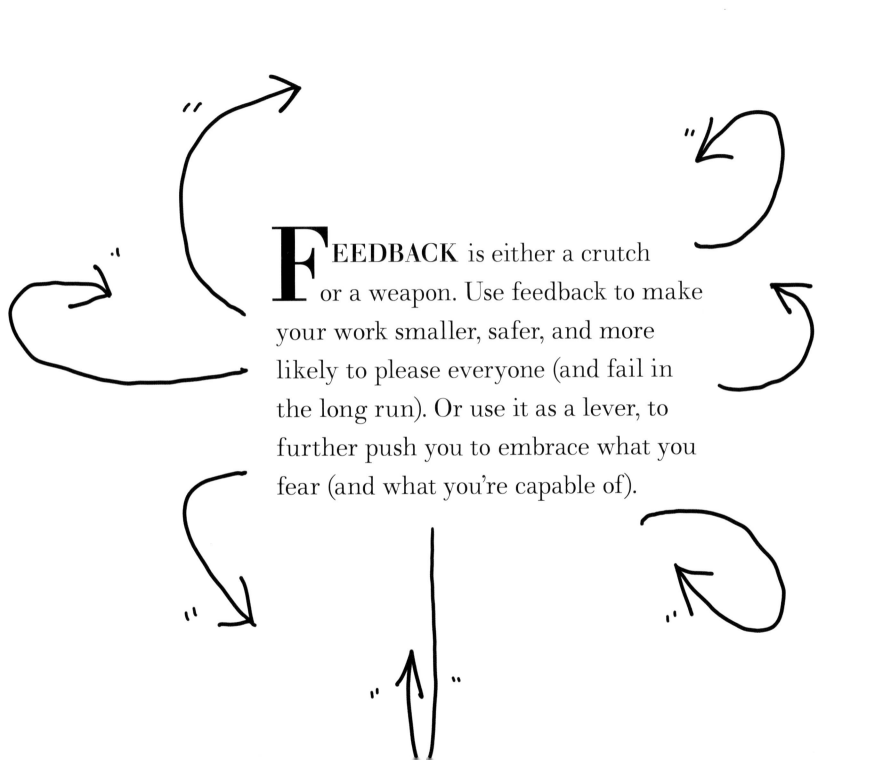

FEEDBACK is either a crutch or a weapon. Use feedback to make your work smaller, safer, and more likely to please everyone (and fail in the long run). Or use it as a lever, to further push you to embrace what you fear (and what you're capable of).

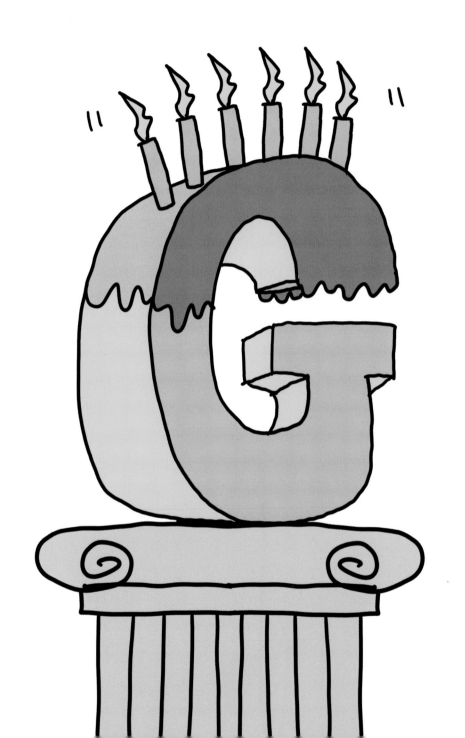

GIFTS are the essence of art. Art isn't made as part of an even exchange, it is your chance to create imbalance, which leads to connection. To share your art is a requirement of making it.

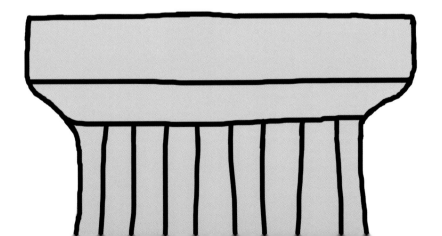

HEROES are people who take risks for the right reasons. Real art is a heroic act. Hipsters, on the other hand, are pretenders who haven't risked a thing but like to play the part.

INITIATIVE is the privilege of picking yourself. You're not given initiative, you take it. Pick yourself. If you're not getting what you want, it may be because you're not making good enough art, often enough.

JOY is different from pleasure or delight or fun. Joy is the satisfaction of connection, the well-earned emotion you deserve after shipping art that made a difference.

A **K**NIFE works best when it has an edge. To take the edge off, to back off, to play it safe, to smooth it out, to please the uninterested masses—it's not what the knife is for.

L is for **LMNO**, which used to be a single letter of the alphabet. The artist seeks to break apart the unbreakable and to combine the uncombinable. And L is for lonely, because everyone is, and the artist does the endless work of helping us conquer that loneliness.

More!

MORE is not the goal of the artist. Better is the artist's dream. Better connection is the point of the work. More stuff leads to a world of scarcity, while better connected creates abundance.

No feels safe, while yes is dangerous indeed. Yes to possibility and yes to risk and yes to looking someone in the eye and telling her the truth.

ONE-BUTTOCK playing is what Ben Zander would have you do. To play the piano and mean it. To sit up, to lean in, to perform as if this was your very best, your very last chance to let the song inside of you get out.

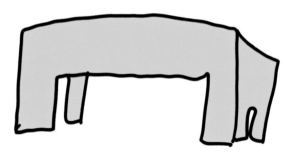

PAIN is the truth of art. Art is not a hobby or a pastime. It is the result of an internal battle royal, one between the quest for safety and the desire to matter.

QUALITY, like feedback, is a trap. To focus on reliably meeting specifications (a fine definition of quality) is to surrender the real work, which is to matter. Quality of performance is a given, it's not the point.

REMIX, reuse, respect, recycle, revisit, reclaim, revere, resorb. Art doesn't repeat itself, but it rhymes.

SHAME is the flip side of vulnerability. We avoid opening ourselves to the connection art brings because we fear that we will finally be seen as the fraud that we are.

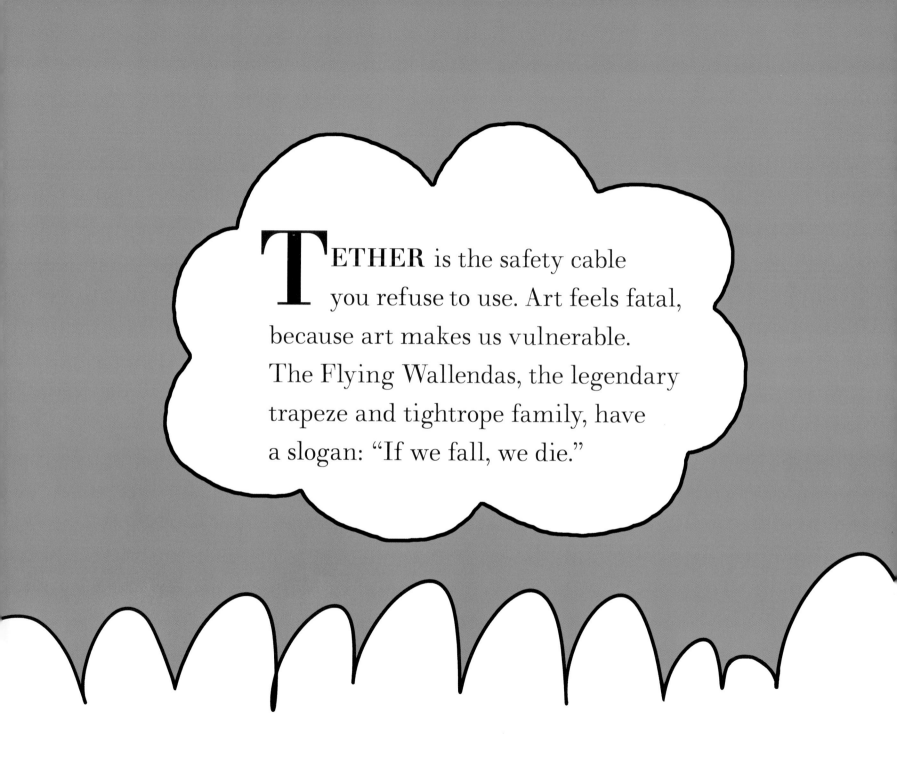

TETHER is the safety cable you refuse to use. Art feels fatal, because art makes us vulnerable. The Flying Wallendas, the legendary trapeze and tightrope family, have a slogan: "If we fall, we die."

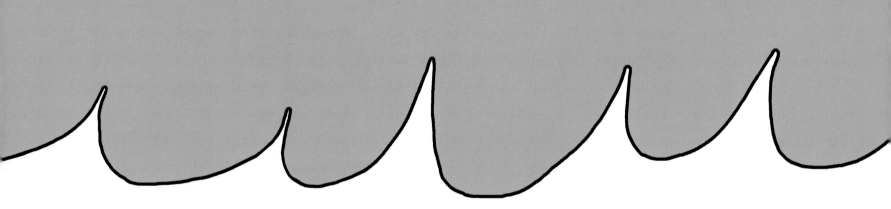

UMBRELLAS keep you from getting wet. Why on earth would you use one? Getting wet is the entire point.

VULNERABLE is the only way we can feel when we truly share the art we've made. When we share it, when we connect, we have shifted all the power and made ourselves naked in front of the person we've given the gift of our art to. We have no excuses, no manual to point to, no standard operating procedure to protect us. And that is part of our gift.

The **W**ARRANTY of merchantability is a legal principle that guarantees that something you buy will do what the seller promises it will. Your work in art doesn't come with one. Your art might not work and your career might not work either. If it doesn't work today, it might not work tomorrow either. But our practice is to persist until it does.

XEBEC is a pirate ship. The real kind, not the sort that selfish, evil, violent pretend pirates in Somalia use. Artist pirates steal in order to remix and then give back.

boink!

YOUTH isn't a number, it's an attitude. So many disruptive artists have been youngsters, even the old ones. Art isn't a genetic or chronological destiny, it's a choice, open to anyone willing to trade pain in exchange for magic.

ZABAGLIONE is a delightful Italian dessert consisting mostly of well-whipped foam. It takes a lot of effort to make by hand. Each batch comes out a little different from the previous one. It's often delicious. It doesn't last long. It's evanescent. And then you have to (get to) make another batch.

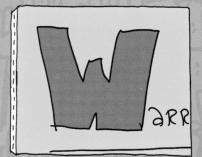

ALSO BY SETH GODIN

The Icarus Deception

Whatcha Gonna Do with That Duck?

Linchpin

Tribes

Meatball Sundae

All Marketers Are Liars

The Dip

Free Prize Inside

Purple Cow

Survival Is Not Enough

Unleashing the Ideavirus

Permission Marketing

Big Red Fez

The Big Moo

Small Is the New Big

Poke the Box

We Are All Weird

SETH GODIN is the author of *The Icarus Deception* and more than a dozen other books. He's also the founder of two successful Internet companies, a popular speaker, and a part-time instructor of style canoeing. The best way to keep up with his ideas is to read his blog (visit sethgodin.com and click on his head).

His favorite picture book is *Hand, Hand, Fingers, Thumb.*

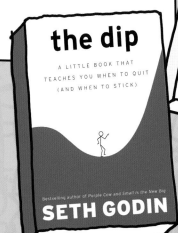

HUGH MACLEOD worked as an advertising copywriter for more than a decade while developing his skills as a cartoonist and pundit. He sells limited edition art and gives away cartoons and ideas at gapingvoid.com. More than four million people have downloaded the original post, "How to Be Creative," which inspired the bestselling book *Ignore Everybody*. He also lectures and consults on Web 2.0 and how it helps a business's purpose and culture. His latest book is *Freedom Is Blogging in Your Underwear*.